SHADING THE COLORS of THE FEMININE ZODIAC

An Adult Coloring Book

by Authors
Lyn Ragan and Dorothy Pigue

Shading The Colors Of The Feminine Zodiac
Copyright © 2016 by Lyn Ragan and Dorothy Pigue

No part of this book shall be reproduced or transmitted in any form or by any means, electronic, mechanical, magnetic, photographic including photocopying, recording or by any information storage and retrieval system, without prior written permission of Lyn Ragan and Dorothy Pigue, except in the case of brief quotations embodied in critical articles and reviews.

No patent liability is assumed with respect to the use of the information contained herein. Although every precaution has been taken in the preparation of this book, the publisher and author assume no responsibility for errors or omissions. Neither is any liability assumed for damages resulting from the use of the information contained herein.

Cover and Book Design by *Lyn M Oney*
Illustrations © Lyn Ragan and Dorothy Pigue
Trade paper ISBN 978-0-9860205-8-2

Any Internet references contained in the work are current at publication time, but the authors cannot guarantee that a specific location will continue to be maintained.

*To our Big and Beautiful Universe,
With Love and Grace...*

Other Books by Lyn Ragan & Dorothy Pigue

Shading The Colors of Grief and Healing
An Adult Coloring Book To Help Heal Through Grief
fb/shadingthecolorsoflife

Coloring The Shades of Grief and Healing
A Teen/Young Adult Coloring Book To Help Heal Through Grief
fb/shadingthecolorsoflife

Shading Spiritual Signs & Symbols
An Adult Coloring Book
fb/shadingthecolorsoflife

Shading The Power Of The Mandala
An Adult Coloring Book
fb/shadingthecolorsoflife

Other Books by Lyn Ragan

Wake Me Up! a true story
How Chip's Afterlife Saved Me
fb/wakemeupbook

We Need To Talk
Living With The Afterlife
fb/weneedtotalkbook

Signs From The Afterlife
Identifying Gifts From The Other Side
fb/signsfromtheafterlife

Signs From Pets In The Afterlife
Identifying Messages From Pets In Heaven
fb/signsfrompetsintheafterlife

Introduction

Lyn Ragan lost the *love of her life* in 2008. One second they were chatting on the phone and in the next, he was killed while preparing for work.

Her grief spiraled into a web of sadness she found difficult to break free of. All of their future dreams destroyed and her life altered forever, Lyn was taken by surprise when she started receiving communications from her deceased fiancé— via dreams. Ms. Ragan would later write about their visits and eventually publish several books on the subject of *Afterlife Communications*.

Her mission in life is to help those who grieve from the loss of a loved one; her ultimate goal to replace painful grief with belief and understanding. Lyn works tirelessly helping those she can reach to understand this physical life is not the end of who we are, and that love and life lives forever— as do our Souls.

Dorothy Pigue was born into a family of clairvoyants. As a young child, she began hearing the voices of spirits around her. It took many years for Dorothy to realize she could communicate with the spirit world and with loved ones who have crossed over. Wanting to enhance her gifts and psychic abilities, she trained with Carl Woodall at the *Atlanta Metaphysical Center* in Atlanta, Georgia, and became a graduate of *The Anastasi System of Psychic Development* in 2014.

Dorothy is also a Master Herbalist who has been practicing as a Korean Medicine Woman since 1996. She is a Clinical Certified Hypnotherapist, a Certified Usui/Holy Fire Reiki ® Practitioner, and an author.

Dorothy's mission in life is to share her gifts and abilities in hopes of removing the *pain of grief*. Healing begins with love and from the other side, *Love* is the message she enjoys sharing.

Authors Lyn Ragan and Dorothy Pigue are excited to come together on a personal undertaking to help bring peace, love, and healing into the hearts of those who grieve.

Understanding the Feminine Zodiac…

*A***strology offers comfort,** faith, and a deeper understanding of the world we live in. Interpretation often provides assurance of one's future but also shows a way to resolve life's issues and improve relationships with family and friends.

The Zodiac is also used as a tool to meet one's self and discover the inner worlds of the Universe in a whole new light.

Each of the twelve horoscope signs belong to one of four elements— Air, Fire, Water and Earth. These elements represent an essential type of energy that acts within each of us. Astrology aims to help us focus these energies on positive aspects in life and gain a better understand of our particular personality profile.

We can associate our astrological sign to almost any aspect in our lives. As we study our individual zodiac sign, we begin to see how insightful and true it is.

Our horoscopes are unique to each of us. They help us find and reveal our strengths, weaknesses, as well as our natural qualities.

Astrology is all about you.

Your horoscope is like a blueprint of your life that was created precisely at the time you were born. That means that your birth chart is as distinctive as your fingerprints or DNA.

Each planet's placement in your horoscope can share a great deal about your personality… and your Destiny.

Aquarius

Aquarius date range:
January 20 — February 18
Symbol: Water Bearer
Planet: Uranus
Element: Air

Lucky numbers: 4, 8, 13, 17, 22, 26
Lucky color: blue, blue-green, grey, black
Lucky day: Saturday, Sunday

Birthstone: Amethyst
Compatibility: Gemini, Libra
Marriage/partnerships: Leo

♒ Aquarius

Aquarius

Likes: A great listener, intellectual conversations, helping others, fighting for causes, having fun with friends and family, being a realist, surprises, social activities

Dislikes: Being lonely, broken promises, limitations, boring people/situations, people who do not agree with them, confrontations, intolerance

Strengths: Independent, humanitarian, original, progressive

Weaknesses: Temperamental, aloof, uncompromising, runs on emotions

Aquarius

Qualities of Aquarius

*If there is no mental stimulation,
they become bored and lack motivation.*

*Aquarius-born have a reputation for being cold
and insensitive, but this is just their way
to defend against being hurt.*

*Aquarius-born are shy and quiet at times,
but are eccentric and energetic as well.
They are deep thinkers and highly intellectual
people who love helping others.*

*Aquarians feel good in a group,
so they constantly strive to be
surrounded by many people.*

Pisces

Pisces date range:
February 19 — March 20
Symbol: Two fish
Planet: Neptune
Element: Water

Lucky numbers: 3, 7, 12, 16, 21, 25, 30, 34, 43, 52
Lucky color: mauve, lilac, purple, violet, sea green
Lucky day: Thursday, Monday

Birthstone: Aquamarine
Compatibility: Cancer, Scorpio
Marriage/partnerships: Virgo

Pisces ♓

Pisces

Likes: Music, romance, sleeping, being alone, swimming, spirituality, daydreaming, helping others, being spontaneous

Dislikes: Cruelty of any kind, being criticized, past coming back, know it alls, rules, facing reality

Strengths: Artistic, intuitive, compassionate, wise, gentle, creative

Weaknesses: Too trusting, sadness, becoming a victim, fearful, desire to escape reality

Pisces ♓

Qualities of Pisces

*Pisces are selfless and always
willing to help others.*

*Their sign is characterized by empathy
and expressed emotional capacity.*

*Pisces are very friendly and enjoy the
company of many different people.*

Pisces are more intuitive and have an artistic talent.

*Pisces are never judgmental and always forgiving.
They are also known to be the most
tolerant of all the zodiac signs.*

Aries

Aries date range:
March 21 — April 19
Symbol: Ram
Planet: Mars
Element: Fire

Lucky numbers: 1,9
Lucky color: red
Lucky day: Tuesday

Birthstone: Diamond
Compatibility: Leo, Sagittarius
Marriage/partnerships: Libra

Aries

Likes: Challenges, sports, leadership roles, comfortable clothing, exploring, being first, taking action

Dislikes: Delays, inactivity, useless work, waiting, having a boss, being ignored, being disappointed

Strengths: Honest, confident, courageous, enthusiastic, optimistic, passionate, determined

Weaknesses: Moody, impulsive, aggressive, impatient, short-tempered

♈ Aries

Qualities of Aries

*Aries is the first sign of the zodiac.
They are always looking for competition.*

*Aries are one of the most active signs
and are always first in everything.*

*Aries seek answers to personal
and metaphysical questions.
They are brave and possess
youthful strength and energy.*

Aries like to work on more than one thing at once.

Taurus

Taurus date range:
April 20 — May 20
Symbol: Bull
Planet: Venus
Element: Earth

Lucky numbers: 2, 4, 6, 11, 20, 29, 37, 47, 56
Lucky color: blue, pink, green
Lucky day: Friday, Monday
Birthstone: Emerald

Compatibility: Virgo, Capricorn
Marriage/partnerships: Scorpio

♉ Taurus

Taurus

<u>Likes</u>: Working with hands, cooking, gardening, romance, music, security, beauty, harmony, good food & drinks, tranquility

<u>Dislikes</u>: Complications, insecurity, sudden changes, being rushed to make decisions, uncomfortable surroundings, aggressive behavior

<u>Strengths</u>: Patient, devoted, responsible, reliable, stable

<u>Weaknesses</u>: Possessive, uncompromising, stubborn

Qualities of Taurus

Taurus loves everything good and beautiful and are often surrounded by material items.

Taurus can be overprotective and jealous at times. They are powerful and reliable and great in making money and they will stick to their projects until it is successfully completed.

Taurus can be an excellent cook, entertainer and artist. They are loyal and do not like sudden and unwanted changes.

Gemini

Gemini date range:
May 21 — June 20
Symbol: Twins
Planet: Mercury
Element: Air

Lucky numbers: 3, 8, 12, 23
Lucky color: green, yellow
Lucky day: Wednesday

Birthstone: Pearl
Compatibility: Libra, Aquarius
Marriage/partnerships: Sagittarius

Gemini

<u>*Likes*</u>: *Conversation, music, magazines, books, short trips around town, solving problems, using their imagination*

<u>*Dislikes*</u>: *Being confined, being alone, routine and repetition, growing old, being bored*

<u>*Strengths*</u>: *Curious, curious, gentle, adaptable, learns quickly*

<u>*Weaknesses*</u>: *Indecisive, inconsistent, nervous*

Gemini ♊

Qualities of Gemini

*Gemini represents two sides of personality.
They are expressive and quick-witted.*

*Gemini's can be sociable, communicative and
ready for fun one second and very serious,
restless and even indecisive the next.*

*Some people born under the Gemini sign
feel like they are missing their other half,
so they are always seeking new friends.*

Cancer

Cancer date range:
June 21 — July 22
Symbol: Crab
Planet: Moon
Element: Water

Lucky numbers: 2, 7, 11, 16, 20, 25
Lucky color: orange, white
Lucky day: Monday, Thursday
Birthstone: Ruby

Compatibility: Scorpio, Pisces
Marriage/partnerships: Capricorn

Cancer

Cancer

<u>Likes</u>: A good meal with friends, helping loved ones, relaxing in or near water, art, home based hobbies, being appreciated, history, money, their home

<u>Dislikes</u>: Revealing of personal life, strangers, criticism, being alone, negative thinking

<u>Strengths</u>: Emotional, loyal, imaginative, sympathetic, persuasive,

<u>Weaknesses</u>: Suspicious, manipulative, insecure, moody, pessimistic

♋ Cancer

Qualities of Cancer

*Cancer is deeply intuitive and sentimental.
They are the most challenging of all the signs.*

*Cancer is very sensitive and emotional
and they care about family and the home.*

*Cancer is sympathetic and is very attached
to the people who surround them.
They are very empathetic people and are able
to empathize with their pain and suffering.
They are deeply intuitive and sentimental.*

*Cancer doesn't have great ambitions, because
they are happy and content to have a loving family
and harmonious home.*

Leo

Leo date range:
July 23 — August 22
Symbol: Lion
Planet: Sun
Element: Fire

Lucky numbers: 1, 4, 10, 13, 19, 22
Lucky color: gold, orange, white, red
Lucky day: Sunday

Birthstone: Peridot
Compatibility: Aries, Sagittarius
Marriage/partnerships: Aquarius

Leo

<u>Likes</u>: Being admired, expensive things, vacations, theater, bright colors, fun with friends, giving advise, loyalty, taking risks, flattery

<u>Dislikes</u>: Facing difficult reality, being told what to do, being ignored, not being treated like a king or queen, boredom, pettiness, being dependent on others

<u>Strengths</u>: Warm-hearted, cheerful, humorous, creative, passionate, generous

<u>Weaknesses</u>: Self-centered, lazy, inflexible, arrogant, stubborn

Leo

Qualities of Leo

*Leo is a fire sign, which means that he loves life
and expects to have a good time.*

*Leo is able to use his/her mind to solve even
the most difficult problems and take the initiative
in solving various complicated situations.
They are natural born leaders and dramatic,
creative, self-confident, dominant,
and extremely difficult to resist.*

*Leo can achieve anything they want,
whether it's about work or time spent
with family and friends. They often have too
many friends because Leo is very generous and loyal.*

*This zodiac sign can also be arrogant, lazy, and inflexible,
because he assumes that someone else
will clean up after him.*

Virgo

Virgo date range:
August 23 — September 22
Symbol: Virgin/maiden
Planet: Mercury
Element: Earth

Lucky numbers: 5, 14, 23, 32, 41, 50
Lucky color: white, yellow, beige, forest green
Lucky day: Wednesday

Birthstone: Sapphire
Compatibility: Taurus, Capricorn
Marriage/partnerships: Pisces

Virgo

<u>Likes</u>: Books, nature, cleanliness, animals, healthy food, being part of a team, being helpful, being social

<u>Dislikes</u>: Taking center stage, rudeness, asking for help, crowds, careless behavior, being unprepared, disorganization, revealing secrets

<u>Strengths</u>: Kind, hardworking, practical, loyal, analytical

<u>Weaknesses</u>: All work and no play, worry, overly critical, shyness

♍ Virgo

Qualities of Virgo

*Virgos are tender and careful.
They pay attention to the smallest details.*

*Virgos have a deep sense of humanity.
They are very organized and conservative.*

*Virgos always want to serve
and please other people.*

Libra

Libra date range:
September 23 — October 22
Symbol: Scales
Planet: Venus
Element: Air

Lucky numbers: 6, 15, 24, 33, 42, 51, 60
Lucky color: Gemini, Aquarius
Lucky day: Friday

Birthstone: Opal
Compatibility: Gemini, Aquarius
Marriage/partnerships: Aries

♎ Libra

Libra

Likes: Sharing with others, the outdoors, harmony, gentleness, facts, logic, balance, arguments

Dislikes: Loudmouths, conformity, violence, injustice, being wrong, unfairness, crowds, falsehood

Strengths: Gracious, fair-minded, social, cooperative, diplomatic

Weaknesses: Will carry a grudge, self-pity, indecisive, avoids confrontations

♎ Libra

Qualities of Libra

Libra hates being alone and enjoys the company of friends and family. They are peaceful and fair.

Libras can be inspired by interesting people and good books. They are the lover of beautiful things so the quality is always more important than the quantity for people.

Libras are extremely cooperative and work well in teams. They do not indulge in conflict and prefer to keep the peace.

Scorpio

Libra date range:
October 23 — November 21
Symbol: Scorpion
Planet: Pluto
Element: Water

Lucky numbers: 9, 18, 27, 36, 45, 54, 63, 72, 81, 90
Lucky color: scarlet, red, rust
Lucky day: Tuesday

Birthstone: Topaz
Compatibility: Cancer, Pisces
Marriage/partnerships: Taurus

Scorpio ♏

Scorpio

<u>Likes</u>: Longtime friends, teasing, passion, truth, facts, being right, being loyal to others, challenges, mysteries

<u>Dislikes</u>: Passive people, dishonesty, revealing secrets, disloyalty, fearfulness, deceitfulness, mind games

<u>Strengths</u>: Passionate, stubborn, a true friend, resourceful, brave

<u>Weaknesses</u>: Secretive, violent, distrusting, jealous

Scorpio ♏

Qualities of Scorpio

*Scorpio is determined and decisive,
and truth seekers.*

They are passionate and assertive people.

Scorpios make great leaders and live to experience and express emotions. Emotions are very important to Scorpios and they are great secret keepers.

Scorpios hate dishonesty and they can be very jealous and suspicious.

Sagittarius

*Sagittarius date range:
November 22 — December 21*

Symbol: Archer

Planet: Jupiter

Element: Fire

Lucky numbers: 3, 12, 21, 30
Lucky color: violet, purple, red, pink
Lucky day: Thursday

Birthstone: Turquoise
Compatibility: Aries, Leo
Marriage/partnerships: Gemini

Sagittarius

<u>Likes</u>: Being outdoors, freedom, traveling, philosophy, animals, speed, entertaining

<u>Dislikes</u>: Off-the-wall theories, details, clingy people, being constrained, deception, sitting still, being insulted, responsibility

<u>Strengths</u>: Idealistic, great sense of humor, generous

<u>Weaknesses</u>: Will say anything no matter how undiplomatic, promises more than can deliver, very impatient

 Sagittarius

Qualities of Sagittarius

*Sagittarius are extroverts, optimistic
and enthusiastic, and likes changes.
They will do anything to reach their goals.*

*Sagittarius are curious, energetic and hard workers.
They are able to transform their thoughts into actions.*

*Sagittarius possess a great sense of humor and
an intense curiosity. It is important for them to
learn to express themselves in a tolerant
and socially acceptable way.*

Capricorn

Capricorn date range:
December 22 — January 19
Symbol: Goat
Planet: Saturn
Element: Earth

Lucky numbers: 1, 4, 8, 10, 13, 17, 19, 22, 26
Lucky color: brown, grey, black
Lucky day: Saturday

Birthstone: Garnet
Compatibility: Taurus, Virgo
Marriage/partnerships: Cancer

Capricorn ♑

Capricorn

<u>Likes</u>: Quality craftsmanship, family, tradition, music, improving themselves, practical thinkers,

<u>Dislikes</u>: Gossip, being angry, public display of affection, laziness

<u>Strengths</u>: Disciplined, self-control, good managers, perfectionists, responsible, business minded

<u>Weaknesses</u>: Condescending, expecting the worst, know-it-all, unforgiving

Capricorn ♑

Qualities of Capricorn

Capricorn is considered the most serious of all the signs. They are professional with traditional values, are independent and great business people.

Capricorns are hard workers and obsessed with being perfect. They are the masters of self-control and are great leaders. They know how to plan and save for the future.

Capricorns can be very stubborn and are masters of proving that they are right. They love to work independently and have a hard time working as a team.

Capricorns can be very controlling and too independent at times.